# TRINIDAD AND TOBAGO 2016 HUMAN RIGHTS REPORT

## EXECUTIVE SUMMARY

The Republic of Trinidad and Tobago is a parliamentary democracy governed by a prime minister and a bicameral legislature.  The island of Tobago's House of Assembly has some administrative autonomy over local matters.  In September 2015 elections, which observers considered generally free and fair, the opposition People's National Movement, led by Keith Rowley, defeated the ruling People's Partnership, led by Kamla Persad-Bissessar, and the political transition was smooth.

Civilian authorities maintained effective control over the security forces.

The most serious human rights problems were police mistreatment of suspects, detainees, and prisoners; poor prison conditions and a slow judicial system; and violence and discrimination against women.

Other human rights problems involved high-profile cases of alleged bribery and corruption; inadequate services for vulnerable populations, such as children and persons with disabilities; and laws that discriminate against lesbian, gay, bisexual, transgender, and intersex (LGBTI) persons.

The government took some steps to punish security force members and other officials charged with killings or other abuse, but there continued to be a perception of impunity based on the open-ended nature of many investigations and the generally slow pace of criminal judicial proceedings.

## Section 1. Respect for the Integrity of the Person, Including Freedom from:

### a. Arbitrary Deprivation of Life and other Unlawful or Politically Motivated Killings

There were no reports that the government or its agents committed arbitrary or unlawful killings.  According to official figures, police shot and killed 16 persons through October 6, compared with 14 in 2015.  Police acknowledged the shooting deaths, but there were occasional discrepancies between the official reporting of shooting incidents and the claims made by witnesses.

## b. Disappearance

There were no reports of politically motivated disappearances.

## c. Torture and Other Cruel, Inhuman, or Degrading Treatment or Punishment

Although the constitution and the law prohibit such practices, there were credible reports that police officers and prison guards mistreated individuals under arrest or in detention.

Officials from the Police Complaints Authority reported receiving few cases of cruel and inhuman treatment.

Andrew Lewis claimed that in February 2015 he was beaten and burned with hot water while in police custody.  Although the Trinidad and Tobago Police Service stated it sent the case file to the Office of the Director of Public Prosecution (DPP) in April 2015, two months later the DPP indicated it was awaiting receipt of the file.

### Prison and Detention Center Conditions

Conditions in some of the prison system's nine facilities continued to be harsh.  In June several inmates at the women's prison went on a hunger strike to protest their living conditions.

Physical Conditions:  Convicted inmates constituted approximately 37 percent of the country's prison population, while the remainder were in pretrial status.  Most prisons suffered from extreme overcrowding, while the maximum-security prison was not at full capacity.  Observers often described the Port of Spain Prison, the remand prison, and the immigration detention center as having particularly poor conditions and severe overcrowding, with as many as nine prisoners kept in cells of 80 square feet.  The Port of Spain Prison, designed to hold 250 inmates, held 610, and the remand prison, designed to hold 655 inmates, held 1,071.  By contrast, the maximum-security prison held inmates in three-person cells, each with a toilet and shower.

The Port of Spain and Remand Prisons had particularly poor lighting, ventilation, and sanitation facilities.

Although conditions at the women's prison were better than those in the Port of Spain and Remand prisons, the women's facility occasionally became overcrowded, since it held both women on remand and those serving prison sentences. The daily average female prison population was 130 in facilities with a maximum capacity of 158. Since there was no female youth facility, authorities placed some underage female prisoners in a segregated wing of the women's prison and returned others to their families.

Media reported that in September, approximately 30 prisoners were allegedly restrained using tie-straps and made to lie on the cold hard floor as a form of retaliation following a protest of harsh conditions at the women's prison. Senior prison officials denied the claims of mistreatment and said they employed force necessary to ensure compliance when prisoners became agitated while officers carried out contraband searches.

Authorities held a daily average of 10 female juveniles at the women's prison. Observers raised concerns that the prison held young girls who had not committed any offense but who were merely in state custody.

The government also operated the Immigration Detention Center, where detainees were irregular immigrants waiting to be deported. The average length of detention was one week to two months, depending on the speed with which the government secured public funding for deportation, as well as transit passports and visas. In some cases detention lasted more than four years. Observers reported that the men's section was overcrowded.

Prisoner abuse and medical neglect were problems.

Administration: Most prisoners could observe their religious practices. Independent authorities investigated and monitored prison and detention center conditions but did not document the results in a publicly accessible manner.

Independent Monitoring: The government permitted regular and open prison visits by UN officials and independent human rights observers upon approval of the Ministry of Justice. These observers enjoyed a reasonable degree of independence.

Improvements: The prison service improved the security of its prison facilities through the purchase of equipment that prevents inmates from illegal use of mobile phones. The prison service also continued to work to improve and expand its K-9 team to stop contraband from entering prisons.

## d. Arbitrary Arrest or Detention

The constitution and the law prohibit arbitrary arrest and detention. Reports of abuses by police remained under investigation at year's end.

The Anti-Gang Act bans membership in criminal gangs and gang-related activities as defined within the statute and permits authorities to hold suspects detained under the law without being charged for up to 120 days, after which the suspect may apply to a judge for bail if the case has not yet reached trial. Authorities continued to arrest many individuals pursuant to the antigang law but subsequently released most arrestees.

Many lawsuits filed in 2012 by some of the approximately 450 suspects detained during the 2011 state of emergency remained pending before the courts with no recent action.

## Role of the Police and Security Apparatus

The Ministry of National Security oversees the police service, immigration division, and defense force, which includes the coast guard. The police service maintains internal security, while the defense force is responsible for external security but also has certain domestic security responsibilities. The coast guard is the main authority responsible for border security along the coastlines where there are no official ports of entry. The Customs and Excise Division and the Immigration Division are responsible for security at the ports. Members of the defense force often joined police officers in patrolling high-crime neighborhoods. Defense force members do not have arrest authority, apart from the coast guard, which can arrest in territorial waters and the Southern Caribbean.

The independent Police Service Commission, in consultation with the prime minister, appoints a commissioner of police to oversee the police force, although there has not been a permanent commissioner assigned since 2012. The commission also makes hiring and firing decisions in the police service, and the ministry typically has little direct influence over changes in senior positions. The Police Service Commission has the power to dismiss police officers, the commissioner of police can suspend officers, and the police service handles the prosecution of officers. Municipal police under the jurisdiction of 14 regional administrative bodies supplement the national police force. Public confidence in police was very low because of high crime rates and perceived corruption.

The Police Complaints Authority (PCA) is a civilian oversight body that investigates complaints about the conduct of police officers, including fatal police shootings; however, it received insufficient funding and had limited investigative authority.  The PCA is free by law from the direction or control of any other person in the performance of its functions.  The PCA had 20 investigators, and from October 1, 2015, through August 16, 2016, the unit received 320 complaints.  Through investigations by the PCA and other bodies, authorities charged police officers with a number of offenses, including attempted murder, corruption, and kidnapping.  The Police Professional Standards Unit and the Police Complaints Division, both nonindependent bodies within the police service, also investigate complaints against police.

**Arrest Procedures and Treatment of Detainees**

A police officer may arrest a person based on a warrant issued or authorized by a magistrate, or without a warrant if the officer witnesses the commission of an alleged offense.  Detainees, as well as those summoned to appear before a magistrate, must appear in court within 48 hours.  In cases of more serious offenses, the magistrate either commits the accused to prison on remand or allows the accused to post bail, pending a preliminary inquiry.  Authorities granted detainees immediate access to a lawyer and to family members.

Ordinarily, bail was available for minor charges.  Persons charged with murder, treason, piracy, kidnapping for ransom, and hijacking, as well as persons convicted twice of violent crimes, are ineligible for bail for a period of up to 120 days following the charge, but a judge may grant bail to such persons under exceptional circumstances.  When authorities denied bail, magistrates advised the accused of their right to an attorney and, with few exceptions, allowed them access to an attorney once they were in custody and prior to interrogation.

The minister of national security may authorize preventive detention to preclude actions prejudicial to public safety, public order, or national defense, in which case the minister must state the grounds for the detention.

Arbitrary Arrest:  False arrest, although infrequent, occurred.  Victims may pursue legal redress and the right to a fair trial through an independent judiciary.

Pretrial Detention:  Lengthy pretrial detention resulting from heavy court backlogs and inefficiencies in the judicial system continued to be a problem.  Pretrial detainees or remand prisoners represented approximately 63 percent of the prison population.  Most persons under indictment waited seven to 10 years for their trial dates in the High Court, although some waited much longer.  Officials cited several reasons for the backlog, including an understaffed and underfunded prosecutorial office, a shortage of defense attorneys for indigent persons, and the burden of the preliminary inquiry process.  Additionally, the law requires anyone charged and detained to appear in person for a hearing before a magistrate's court every 10 days, if only to have the case postponed for an additional 10 days, resulting in further inefficiency.

<u>Detainee's Ability to Challenge Lawfulness of Detention before a Court</u>:  Persons who believe they have been arrested or detained in unfair circumstances may bring an action for malicious prosecution, which offers persons a legal basis to challenge the arbitrary nature of their detention and obtain prompt release and compensation if found to have been unlawfully detained.

## e. Denial of Fair Public Trial

The constitution and the law provide for an independent judiciary, whose operation the government generally respected.  Although the judicial process was generally fair, it was slow due to backlogs and inefficiencies.  Prosecutors and judges stated that witness and jury intimidation remained a problem.

## Trial Procedures

The constitution and the law provide all defendants with the right to a fair trial, and an independent judiciary generally enforced this right.  Magistrates try both minor and more serious offenses, but in the latter cases, the magistrate must conduct a preliminary inquiry.  Trials are public.  Defendants have the right to be present, are presumed innocent until proven guilty, and have the right to appeal.  Authorities inform them promptly and in detail of all charges.  All defendants have the right to consult with an attorney in a timely manner and have adequate time and facilities to prepare a defense.  Authorities provide an attorney at public expense to defendants facing serious criminal charges, and the law requires provision of an attorney to any person accused of murder.  Although the courts may appoint attorneys for indigent persons charged with serious crimes, an indigent person may refuse to accept an assigned attorney for cause and may obtain a replacement.  Defendants can confront or question adverse witnesses, present witnesses and evidence on their own behalf, and access government-held evidence relevant to their cases.  Defendants may not be compelled to testify or confess guilt.  The government provides free foreign language as well as sign-language interpreters as necessary in court cases.

Both civil and criminal appeals may be filed with the Court of Appeal and ultimately with the Privy Council in the United Kingdom.

**Political Prisoners and Detainees**

There were no reports of political prisoners or detainees.

**Civil Judicial Procedures and Remedies**

Individuals or organizations are free to file lawsuits against civil breaches of human rights in both the High Court and petty civil court.  The High Court may review the decisions of lower courts, order parties to cease and desist from particular actions, compel parties to take specific actions, and award damages to aggrieved parties.  Court cases may be appealed to the Inter-American Commission on Human Rights.

**f. Arbitrary or Unlawful Interference with Privacy, Family, Home, or Correspondence**

The constitution and the law prohibit such actions, and there were no reports that the government failed to respect these prohibitions.

**Section 2. Respect for Civil Liberties, Including:**

**a. Freedom of Speech and Press**

The constitution and the law provide for freedom of speech and press, and the government generally respected these rights.  An independent press, an effective judiciary, and a functioning democratic political system combined to promote freedom of speech and press.

Freedom of Speech and Expression:  The law prohibits acts that would offend or insult another person or group on the basis of race, origin, or religion or that would incite racial or religious hatred.

<u>Violence and Harassment</u>:  Unlike in 2015 there were no credible reports of journalists being arrested, imprisoned, attacked, or intimidated by any actor due to their reporting.

<u>Censorship or Content Restrictions</u>:  Unlike in 2015 there were no credible reports of the government penalizing those who published items counter to government guidelines or directly or indirectly censoring the media.

**Internet Freedom**

The government did not restrict or disrupt access to the internet or censor online content, and there were no credible reports that the government monitored private online communications without appropriate legal authority.  According to the International Telecommunication Union, 65 percent of citizens used the internet in 2014.

**Academic Freedom and Cultural Events**

There were no government restrictions on academic freedom or cultural events.

**b. Freedom of Peaceful Assembly and Association**

The constitution and the law provide for the freedoms of assembly and association, and the government generally respected these rights.

**c. Freedom of Religion**

See the Department of State's *International Religious Freedom Report* at www.state.gov/religiousfreedomreport/.

**d. Freedom of Movement, Internally Displaced Persons, Protection of Refugees, and Stateless Persons**

The constitution and various laws provide for freedom of internal movement, foreign travel, emigration, and repatriation, and the government generally respected these rights.

The government cooperated with the Office of the UN High Commissioner for Refugees (UNHCR) and other humanitarian organizations in providing protection and assistance to refugees, returning refugees, asylum seekers, stateless persons, or other persons of concern.

<u>Abuse of Migrants, Refugees, and Stateless Persons</u>:  There were isolated claims of sexual harassment and exploitation of refugees who worked in the informal economy.

**Protection of Refugees**

<u>Access to Asylum</u>:  The government has not passed legislation to implement its obligations under the 1951 UN Convention and its 1967 Protocol Relating to the Status of Refugees.  As a result, the law does not provide for the granting of refugee status.  The law does not provide for any exemption or penalization of irregular entry of asylum seekers.  Persons who indicate a need for international protection may be subject to detention, criminal proceedings, and conviction of the crime of illegal entry; however, in practice refugees lived throughout the country, worked illegally, and sent their children to local public schools.

In the absence of national legislation, UNHCR registers all asylum seekers, conducts refugee status determination on behalf of the government, and promotes durable solutions for all refugees recognized under UNHCR's mandate.  The Living Water Community (LWC), a local Roman Catholic nongovernmental organization (NGO) and UNHCR's operational partner, is the first point of contact for persons of concern to UNHCR.  It provides orientation and counseling and notifies the Immigration Division of the respective asylum applications.  In close coordination with UNHCR, the LWC engages in case management and provides psychosocial care and humanitarian assistance, including cash, housing assistance, and legal aid, among other services.

Pending parliament's approval of implementing legislation, the Ministry of National Security's Immigration Division authorizes the stay of asylum seekers and refugees through the issuance of orders of supervision, but these measures do not guarantee refugees and asylum seekers the rights they are entitled to under the 1951 convention.

<u>Refoulement</u>:  Due to a lack of training and awareness of refugee rights by officers at points of entry, there were at least four instances of refoulement in the first half of the year.

<u>Employment</u>:  Refugees are not permitted to work.  There were isolated claims of sexual harassment and exploitation of refugees who worked in the informal economy.

<u>Access to Basic Services</u>:  Refugee children had access to education, although there were reports of difficulties in enrolling them in public schools due to insufficient spaces and other practical obstacles.  Refugees had access to most health-care services.  They did not have access to identity documents and surrendered their passports to the Immigration Division.

<u>Durable Solutions</u>:  Due to the absence of national legislation that would allow for local integration, resettlement continued to be the main durable solution for refugees in the country.  UNHCR, the LWC, and the International Organization of Migration collaborated on the identification, submission, and transfer of refugees in need of resettlement.  In the first half of the year, 25 individuals were resettled to a third country, mostly to the United States.

The government also closely collaborated with UNHCR by facilitating the resettlement of a few refugees recognized under UNHCR's mandate in smaller Caribbean islands by allowing them to stay temporarily in the country to complete the formalities required for resettlement and then directly travel to their new asylum country.

<u>Temporary Protection</u>:  The government provided temporary protection to some Syrian refugees on an order of supervision, which allows free, legal movement, so long as refugees complete periodic visits to immigration officials.  The LWC reported that many Cubans who filed petitions eventually abandoned their applications and left the country or simply walked away from the LWC because of the often-lengthy processing time and the lack of rights, particularly the right to work.

**Section 3. Freedom to Participate in the Political Process**

The constitution and the law provide citizens the ability to choose their government in free and fair periodic elections held by secret ballot and based on universal and equal suffrage.

**Elections and Political Participation**

<u>Recent Elections</u>:  In September 2015 elections, the opposition People's National Movement, led by Keith Rowley, defeated the ruling People's Partnership, led by Kamla Persad-Bissessar, winning 23 parliamentary seats to the Partnership's 18 seats.  Commonwealth observers considered the elections generally free and fair.  During the campaign, however, observers noted the "lack of transparency and accountability regarding the financing of political parties."  Many experts raised concerns that the lack of campaign finance rules gives any incumbent party an advantage.

Following the election former prime minister Persad-Bissessar initiated a court challenge to overturn the election results.  The former prime minister challenged the results in six key swing constituencies where the results were close and where the People's Partnership argued that a last-minute decision by the Elections and Boundaries Commission to extend voting helped the opposition.  The courts found that the commission was wrong to extend voting but that this action did not change the results of the election.

<u>Participation of Women and Minorities</u>:  No laws limit participation of women and minorities in the political process, and women and minorities did so.  There were 13 women in the Lower House and nine in the Upper House.  Women served in senior positions including opposition leader, speaker of the assembly, president of the senate, and head seven government ministries.

## Section 4. Corruption and Lack of Transparency in Government

The law provides criminal penalties for corruption by officials, but the government did not implement the law effectively, and officials sometimes engaged in corrupt practices.  There were reports of government corruption during the year, and the 2016-17 World Economic Forum *Global Competitiveness Report* ranked corruption as the second-most problematic factor to doing business in the country.  There were no documented instances of individuals receiving a criminal punishment for alleged corruption.

<u>Corruption</u>:  Corruption in the police and immigration services continued to be a problem, with senior officials acknowledging that officers participated in corrupt and illegal activities.  There were allegations that some police officers had close relationships with gang leaders and that police, customs, and immigration officers often accepted bribes to facilitate drug, weapons, and human smuggling and trafficking.  There is no internal affairs unit responsible for investigating incidents of professional misconduct attributed to law enforcement officials.

In August, two police officers were arrested and charged with taking bribes. The two men allegedly were paid approximately $1,270 Trinidad and Tobago dollars (TTD) ($190) to forgo arresting a man. The officers were charged and released on bail.

There were continued allegations that some ministers used their positions for personal gain. A government minister was removed as minister during a corruption investigation. No charges were made, and she retained her parliamentary seat.

Financial Disclosure: The law mandates that public officials disclose their assets, income, and liabilities to the Integrity Commission, which monitors, verifies, and publishes disclosures. Officials and candidates for public office were reluctant to comply with asset disclosure rules, primarily because of the perceived invasiveness of the process. The act stipulates a process when public officials fail to disclose assets and provides criminal penalties for failure to comply. The law clearly states which assets, liabilities, and interests public officials must declare.

While the commission undertook numerous investigations, it seldom referred cases to law enforcement authorities, and prosecution of those officials who refused to comply with asset disclosure rules was very limited. The Integrity Commission experienced turnover in its leadership positions and staffing shortages, and the media and public regularly raised questions about its effectiveness.

Public Access to Information: The law provides for public access to government documents. It includes a sufficiently narrow list of exceptions outlining the grounds for nondisclosure, although some critics charged that authorities exempted a growing number of public bodies from the law's coverage. The law has an appeal mechanism for review of disclosure denials. Critics also noted the law does not have an enforcement mechanism if the government does not respond within the prescribed 30-day period. Criminal penalties, including imprisonment, exist for those who destroy documents of record, but there are no sanctions or other penalties for officials who do not comply with the procedural requirements of the law. The government maintained an easily navigable website on how to use the law effectively

**Section 5. Governmental Attitude Regarding International and Nongovernmental Investigation of Alleged Violations of Human Rights**

A number of domestic and international human rights groups generally operated without government restriction, investigating human rights cases and publishing their findings.  Government officials generally were cooperative and responsive to their views.

Government Human Rights Bodies:  The ombudsman investigates citizens' complaints concerning the administrative decisions of government agencies.  Where there is evidence of a breach of duty, misconduct, or criminal offense, the ombudsman may refer the matter to the appropriate authority.  The ombudsman has a quasi-autonomous status within the government and publishes a comprehensive annual report.  Both the public and the government had confidence in the integrity and reliability of the Office of the Ombudsman and the ombudsman's annual report.

**Section 6. Discrimination, Societal Abuses, and Trafficking in Persons**

**Women**

Rape and Domestic Violence:  Rape, including spousal rape, is illegal and punishable by up to life imprisonment, but the courts often imposed considerably shorter sentences.  The government and NGOs reported that many incidents of rape and other sexual crimes were unreported, partly due to perceived insensitivity of police, exacerbated by a wide cultural acceptance of gender-based violence.  Data from the Crime and Problem Analysis branch of the police service revealed that there were approximately 11,441 reports related to domestic violence between 2010 and 2015, 75 percent of these reports pertained to women.  For the same period, 56 percent of 131 domestic violence-related deaths were women.  Police channeled resources to its Victim and Witness Support Unit in an effort to overcome the problem.  The unit continued outreach activities to support survivors of domestic violence.  Police recruits also received additional training in the handling of domestic violence cases, and the service introduced new questions relating to domestic violence legislation to basic training exams.

Many community leaders asserted that violence against women, particularly in the form of domestic violence, continued to be a significant problem.  The law provides for protection orders separating perpetrators of domestic violence, including abusive spouses and common-law partners, from their victims.  Courts may also fine or imprison abusive spouses, but it was rarely done.  While reliable national statistics were not available, women's groups estimated that as many as 50 percent of all women suffered abuse.

The NGO Coalition against Domestic Violence charged that police often hesitated to enforce domestic violence laws and asserted that rape and sexual abuse against women and children remained a serious and pervasive problem.

Two NGOs, the Domestic Violence Unit and the Rape Crisis Society, received funding from the government and operated a 24-hour hotline for victims of domestic violence. Hotline operators referred callers to NGO-run shelters for female victims, a rape crisis center, counseling services, support groups, and other assistance providers.

Sexual Harassment: No laws specifically prohibit sexual harassment. Although related statutes could be used to prosecute perpetrators of sexual harassment, and some trade unions incorporated antiharassment provisions in their contracts, both the government and NGOs continued to suspect that many incidents of sexual harassment went unreported.

Reproductive Rights: Couples and individuals have the right to decide the number, spacing, and timing of their children; manage their reproductive health; and have access to the information and means to do so, free from discrimination, coercion, or violence. Sexual health education is not a part of the national school curriculum, and barriers to access to contraception included cost, availability, and locality.

Discrimination: Women generally enjoyed the same legal status and rights as men. No laws or regulations require equal pay for equal work. While equal pay for men and women in public service was the rule rather than the exception, both the government and NGOs noted considerable disparities in pay between men and women in the private and informal sectors, particularly in agriculture.

**Children**

Birth Registration: Every person born in the country is a citizen at birth, unless the parents are foreign envoys accredited to the country. Children born outside the country can become citizens at birth if on that date one or both of the parents is, or was, a citizen. The law requires registration of every child born alive within 42 days of birth. Any person who registers or causes to be registered the birth of any child in contravention to the Births and Deaths Registration Act is liable to a fine of $1,000 TTD ($150).

Child Abuse:  Child abuse cases continued to increase; during the Children's Authority's first nine months of operations ending February 17, a total of 4,158 children were brought to the authority's attention.  Of those, 915 cases were found to be sexual abuse, and 87 percent of the victims were female.  The Children's Authority has the power to receive and investigate reports of child abuse, remove children from their homes if they are deemed to be in imminent danger, and provide for foster homes around the country to be inspected and properly licensed.  The Children's Authority also has full responsibility for the country's foster care and adoption system.  The Ministry of Gender, Youth, and Child Development reported that young schoolchildren were vulnerable to rape, physical abuse, and drug use; some had access to weapons or lived with drug-addicted parents.

ChildLine, in partnership with the Ministry of Education, operated the National Student Hotline, a free and confidential round-the-clock telephone hotline for at-risk or distressed children and young adults up to age 25.  ChildLine referred all calls relating to physical or sexual abuse to police or to social service agencies.

The law prohibits both corporal punishment of children and sentencing a child to prison.  According to NGOs, however, abuse of children in their own homes or in institutional settings remained a serious problem, but there were no reliable statistics on prevalence.

Early and Forced Marriage:  Although the legal age for civil and Christian marriage is 18 for both men and women, the distinct laws and attitudes of the various religious denominations determine the minimum legal age for marriage.  Under the Muslim Marriage and Divorce Act, the minimum legal age for marriage is 16 for men and 12 for women; under the Hindu Marriage Act, the minimum legal age for marriage is 18 for men and 14 for women; and under the Orisa Marriage Act, the minimum legal age for marriage is 18 for men and 16 for women.  Statistics from the Office of the Registrar General showed an increase in child marriages over the past two decades, with 548 certified marriages of children between the ages of 12 and 16 occurring during the 10-year period 2006-16.

Sexual Exploitation of Children:  The law defines a child as less than 18 years of age.  The age of sexual consent is 18, and the age of consent for sexual touching is 16.  Sexual penetration of a child is punishable by a maximum of life in prison.  The law decriminalizes sexual exploration between minors close in age but specifically retains language criminalizing the same activity among same-sex minors, although this was not enforced.  The law also creates specific offenses such as sexual grooming of a child (gaining the trust of a child, or of a person who takes care of the child, for the purpose of sexual activity with the child) and child pornography.  The 2012 Children Act, which entered into force in May 2015, prescribes penalties of 10 years' to life imprisonment for subjecting a child to prostitution.

International Child Abductions:  The government is a party to the 1980 Hague Convention on the Civil Aspects of International Child Abduction.  See the Department of State's *Annual Report on International Parental Child Abduction* at travel.state.gov/content/childabduction/en/legal/compliance.html.

**Anti-Semitism**

There were fewer than 100 Jews in the country.  There were no reports of any anti-Semitic acts.

**Trafficking in Persons**

See the Department of State's *Trafficking in Persons Report* at www.state.gov/j/tip/rls/tiprpt/.

**Persons with Disabilities**

The government formed a committee to implement the Convention on the Rights of Persons with Disabilities (CRPD), which it ratified in June 2015, but only one person with a disability was included on the committee.  Disability rights advocates were aware of no efforts by the government to implement the CRPD.  Prior to the ratification of the convention, the law prohibited discrimination on the basis of disability but did not mandate equal access for persons with disabilities to the political process, employment, education, transportation, housing, health care, the judicial system, or provision of other citizen services.

Persons with disabilities faced a number of obstacles to participating in the 2015 national elections, including a lack of physical access for persons with disabilities and sign language interpreting at political rallies.  Voting stations for the most part were not accessible to persons with disabilities.  No persons with disabilities participated as candidates or election officials.

Persons with disabilities faced discrimination and denial of opportunities.  Such discrimination could be traced to architectural barriers, employers' reluctance to make necessary accommodations that would enable otherwise qualified job candidates to work, an absence of support services to assist students with disabilities to study, lowered expectations of the abilities of persons with disabilities, condescending attitudes, and disrespect.

The Bureau of Standards adopted standards to make public buildings more accessible to persons with disabilities, although it had not developed a larger strategy for retrofitting existing public buildings.

Accessible parking spaces are provided voluntarily and not enforced by laws. Parking space placards and eligibility requirements do not exist, outside of those created by a local grocery store chain.

**Indigenous People**

The census did not record indigenous people as a distinct group, although a very small group of persons identified themselves as descendants of the country's original Amerindian population. The government effectively protected their civil and political rights, and they were not subject to discrimination or violence.

**Acts of Violence, Discrimination, and Other Abuses Based on Sexual Orientation and Gender Identity**

Although the law criminalizes consensual same-sex sexual activity, providing penalties of up to 25 years' imprisonment, the government generally did not enforce such legislation, except in conjunction with more serious offenses such as rape. Immigration laws also bar the entry of "homosexuals" into the country, but the legislation was not enforced during the year.

The law identifying classes of persons protected from discrimination does not prohibit discrimination based on sexual orientation. The 2012 Children Act decriminalizes sexual exploration between minors close in age but specifically retains language criminalizing the same activity among same-sex minors. Other laws exclude same-sex partners from their protections. LGBTI rights groups reported that a stigma related to sexual orientation or gender identity in the country remained and likely inhibited reporting incidents.

In general victims of gay-related hate crimes avoided media attention.

In September, Attorney General Faris al-Rawi appointed a committee to consider amendments to the definition of sex in the Equal Opportunities Act to include sexual orientation.

## HIV and AIDS Social Stigma

UNAIDS estimated there were 11,000 persons with HIV in 2015. HIV/AIDS was a medical and public health concern for the government, and civil society organizations engaged in HIV/AIDS response work. Stigmatization of those with HIV persisted, especially among high-risk groups, including men who have sex with men. There were reports of discrimination against this group, although no clear evidence of any violence. The government's HIV and AIDS Agency and Secretariat coordinates the national response to HIV/AIDS, and the government employed HIV/AIDS coordinators in all ministries as part of its multisector response.

## Section 7. Worker Rights

## a. Freedom of Association and the Right to Collective Bargaining

The law, including related statutes and regulations, provides for the right of most workers, including those in state-owned enterprises, to form and join independent unions, bargain collectively, and conduct legal strikes, but with some limitations. Neither employers nor employees listed in essential services, such as hospital, fire, and external communications (telephone, telegraph, wireless), have the right to strike, and walkouts can bring punishment of up to 36 months in prison and a fine of $40,000 TTD ($5,970). These employees negotiate with the government's chief personnel officer to resolve labor disputes. The law stipulates that only strikes over unresolved interest disputes may take place and that authorities may prohibit strikes at the request of one party if not called by a majority union.

The law also provides for mandatory recognition of a trade union when it represents 51 percent or more of the workers in a specified bargaining unit. The law allows unions to participate in collective bargaining, prohibits employers from dismissing or otherwise prejudicing workers due to their union membership, and mandates reinstatement of workers illegally dismissed for union activities. The government's Registration, Recognition, and Certification Board determines whether a given workers' organization meets the definition of a bargaining unit and can limit union recognition by this means. The Industrial Relations Act definition of a worker excludes domestic workers (house cleaners, chauffeurs, and gardeners), but domestic workers have an established trade union that advocates for their rights.  Separate legislation governs the employment relationship between the government and its employees, including civil servants, teachers, and members of the protective services (fire, police, and prison services).  The Industrial Relations Act prohibits these employees from taking industrial action.  The government effectively enforced applicable laws.

A union must have the support of an absolute majority of workers to obtain bargaining rights.  This limited the right of collective bargaining.  Furthermore, collective agreements must be for a minimum of three years, making it almost impossible for such agreements to cover workers on short-term contracts.  According to the National Trade Union Center, the requirement that all negotiations go through the Public Sector Negotiation Committee rather than through the individual government agency or government-owned industry, provided an additional onerous restriction that added significant delays.  Some unions claimed the government undermined the collective bargaining process by pressuring the committee to offer raises of no more than 5 percent over three years.  The International Labor Organization called for an amendment to the Industrial Relations Act to ensure that in cases in which trade unions do not represent the majority of workers, minority unions can jointly negotiate a collective agreement applicable in a specified bargaining unit, or at least conclude a collective agreement on behalf of their own members.

The government enforced labor laws effectively, including with effective remedies and penalties.  Resources, inspections, and remediation were adequate, although some observers called for an increased number of unannounced inspections and additional industrial court judges.  A union may request that the Industrial Court enforce the laws, and the court may order employers found guilty of antiunion activities or otherwise in violation of the Industrial Relations Act to reinstate workers and pay compensation or may impose other penalties, including imprisonment.  There was no information on specific penalties or whether they were sufficient to deter violations.

Authorities generally respected freedom of association and the right to collective bargaining.  Authorities did not use excessive force to end strikes or protests, or otherwise retaliate against workers seeking to exercise their rights.

### b. Prohibition of Forced or Compulsory Labor

The law prohibits forced and compulsory labor. Upon conviction, perpetrators of forced labor are subject to a fine of at least $500,000 TTD ($74,600) and imprisonment for at least 15 years. Penalties were sufficient to deter violations. The Counter-Trafficking Unit, housed within the Ministry of National Security, is charged with investigating potential forced labor cases and with referring cases for prosecution.

There were no confirmed cases of forced labor, or specific cases reported by NGOs or the media. There were no prosecutions or convictions through October. One of the cases brought to the court in 2015 concluded in the magistrate court, with a decision pending as to whether it would progress to the High Court.

Also see the Department of State's *Trafficking in Persons Report* at www.state.gov/j/tip/rls/tiprpt/.

## c. Prohibition of Child Labor and Minimum Age for Employment

The law sets the minimum age for employment in public and private industries at 16. Children ages 14 to 16 may work in activities in which only family members are employed or that the minister of education approved as vocational or technical training. The law prohibits children under age 18 from working between the hours of 10 p.m. and 5 a.m., except in a family enterprise or within other limited exceptions. There is no clear minimum age for hazardous activities.

Violation of child labor laws is punishable by six months' imprisonment or a fine of $2,500 TTD ($373). In cases of child trafficking, including forced or exploitive child labor, perpetrators are subject to fines of one million TTD ($150,000) and 20 years' imprisonment. These penalties were sufficient to deter violations.

The government was generally effective in enforcing child labor laws, and the penalties were sufficient to deter violations, but there were anecdotal reports of children working in agriculture or as domestic workers. The Ministry of Labor and Small Enterprise Development and the Ministry of the People and Social Development are responsible for enforcing child labor laws. There were 18 labor inspectors in the Labor Inspectorate Unit in 2016, compared with 10 in 2015, trained to investigate and identify cases of child labor and also to identify and report on indicators relating to possible cases of forced labor involving children. The unit recruited eight new labor inspectors in late 2015. They underwent in-house training in child labor. The country also participated in the Regional Initiative Latin America and Caribbean Free of Child Labor.

The minister may designate an inspector to gather information from parents and employers regarding the employment of a person under 18.  The Industrial Court may issue a finding of contempt against anyone obstructing the inspectors' investigation.

The government did not have comprehensive mechanisms for receiving, investigating, and resolving child labor complaints.  There were anecdotal reports of children engaged in the worst forms of child labor in the small-scale agricultural sector, domestic service.

Also see the Department of Labor's *Findings on the Worst Forms of Child Labor* at www.dol.gov/ilab/reports/child-labor/findings/.

## d. Discrimination with Respect to Employment and Occupation

The law and regulations prohibited discrimination with respect to employment and occupation on the basis of race, color, sex, religion, political opinion, national origin or citizenship, and social origin.  The government effectively enforced those laws and regulations.  The law did not prohibit employment discrimination on the basis of political opinion, sexual orientation, gender identity, language, age, disability, or HIV status or other communicable disease.  Discrimination in employment occurred with respect to disability.  No other new legislation was passed in relation to discrimination.

The Equal Opportunity Tribunal found that a Muslim woman was wrongfully terminated from her job for wearing a hijab and awarded her damages.

## e. Acceptable Conditions of Work

The national minimum wage was $15 TTD ($2.24) per hour.

The law establishes a 40-hour workweek, a daily period for lunch or rest, and premium pay for overtime.  The law does not prohibit excessive or compulsory overtime.  The law provides for paid leave, with the amount of leave varying according to length of service.  Workers in the informal economy reported wages above the national minimum wage but reported working more than 40-hour workweeks.

The law sets occupational health and safety standards, which were current and appropriate for the main industries in the country.  The Ministry of Labor and Small Enterprise Development was responsible for enforcing labor laws related to minimum wage and acceptable conditions of work, while the Occupational Safety and Health Agency (OSHA) enforced occupational health and safety regulations, which apply to all workers, regardless of citizenship.  Local labor laws generally protected foreign laborers brought into the country, a stipulation usually contained in their labor contract.  Resources, inspections, and penalties appeared adequate to deter violations.  The Occupational Safety and Health Act provides a range of fines and terms of imprisonment for violations of the law, but despite these penalties a number of violations occurred.  OSHA prosecuted four cases in 2014 and during the year with an average fine of $130,000 TTD ($19,400).  No one was imprisoned over the period.

The Occupational Safety and Health Act provides workers the right to remove themselves from situations that endangered health or safety without jeopardy to their employment, and authorities generally protected this right.  For the period January to July, OSHA reported three on-the-job fatalities, seven critical accidents, and 375 noncritical accidents.